CAREERS THAT COUNT

FIREFIGHTER

FIRE DISTRICT

DEPUTY CHIEF

Louise Spilsbury

PowerKiDS press™

New York

Published in 2016 by **The Rosen Publishing Group**
29 East 21st Street, New York, NY 10010

Produced for Rosen by Calcium

Editors for Calcium: Sarah Eason and Jennifer Sanderson
Designer: Emma DeBanks

Picture credits: Cover: Shutterstock: Fluke Samed (top), Digital Storm (bottom); Inside:
Shutterstock: Baloncici 16, Tatiana Belova 6t, Nathan DeMarse 10, Denisenko 8, 12, 16, 22,
30, 32, Digital Storm 11, DVW Creations 1, 26, EDG 22–23, Flashon Studio 28, Sarah Jessup
19 b, Koka55 15, Patricia Marks 27, Monkey Business Images 12, 24, Nejron Photo 9, NF
Photography 18–19, Anton Oparin 21, Valentina Petrov 20, Phichai 2, Phiseksit 6, 8, 10, 14,
17, 18, 21, 23, 24, 27, Photovova 4, Potowizard 7, Fluke Samed 4, 6b, 8, 10, 11, 12, 16, 18,
20, 22, 24, 26, 28, 30, 32, 31, Jeff Thrower 17, Worradirek 14.

Cataloging-in-Publication Data
Spilsbury, Louise.
Firefighter / by Louise Spilsbury.
p. cm. — (Careers that count)
Includes index.
ISBN 978-1-4994-0805-8 (pbk.)
ISBN 978-1-4994-0804-1 (6 pack)
ISBN 978-1-4994-0803-4 (library binding)
1. Fire extinction — Juvenile literature. 2. Fire fighters — Juvenile literature.
I. Spilsbury, Louise. II. Title.
TH9148.S65 2016
363.37—d23

Manufactured in the United States of America
CPSIA Compliance Information: Batch WS15PK: For Further Information contact Rosen Publishing, New York, New York at 1-800-237-9932

CONTENTS

WHICH CAREERS COUNT?

Police officer, lifeguard, and firefighter, these are all careers that count. Careers like these are special because they make a huge difference in other people's lives. Some people look for a job with a big paycheck, but this will not necessarily make them happy. Studies show that careers that make people happiest are the ones in which workers help others, are creative, or use their knowledge and skills. Workers who do not have any challenges, do not use their skills or knowledge, or do the same thing day after day may often feel bored at work or not enjoy the work they do.

While most people run in the opposite direction of a fire, it is a firefighter's job to face the smoke and flames to rescue anyone trapped by the blaze.

Take the Challenge

If you choose to work in a career that helps others, you will face challenges and difficulties. However, no two days will be the same and you will feel a huge sense of satisfaction when you make a difference in other people's lives. Some people work to improve people's health, help them during difficult times, or teach them new skills. In this book we will look at the work of firefighters, heroes who save lives and property.

Careers That Count: A Career for You?

Here are three things you can do to figure out if a career that counts might be right for you:

- Get to know yourself. What are your strengths, values, interests, and **ambitions**?

- Find out as much as you can about your chosen job and what it is really like. Reading this book is a good place to start.

- Talk to your teachers and a **career adviser**. They might suggest options that you did not know about.

HEROES WHO SAVE LIVES

Being a firefighter is one of the toughest jobs a person can do. A firefighter is trained to save the lives of people in danger, which often means putting his or her own life on the line. A firefighter helps people in many different dangerous situations, like rescuing people from burning buildings and helping those trapped in vehicles during road accidents. On call both day and night, being a firefighter is a job that requires true commitment and courage.

Firefighters are trained to figure out how dangerous a situation is and if they can safely attempt a rescue.

WHAT MAKES A GREAT FIREFIGHTER?

Firefighters follow a long and **rigorous** training program to make sure they are able to safely carry out their role. However, there are also some important **characteristics** all firefighters need to be able to do this dangerous job. Firefighters must be:

- Trustworthy: their team and the public depend on them.
- Able to listen: firefighters must follow instructions.
- Brave: firefighters put the needs of others first.

Which of the above do you think is most important and why?

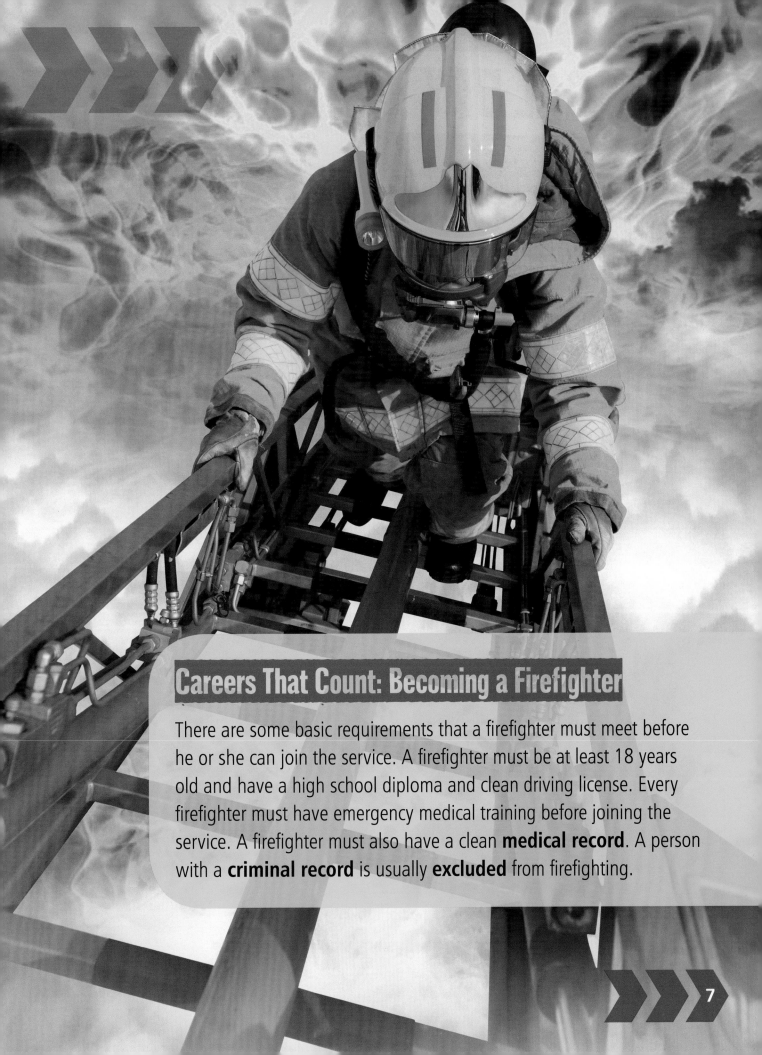

Careers That Count: Becoming a Firefighter

There are some basic requirements that a firefighter must meet before he or she can join the service. A firefighter must be at least 18 years old and have a high school diploma and clean driving license. Every firefighter must have emergency medical training before joining the service. A firefighter must also have a clean **medical record**. A person with a **criminal record** is usually **excluded** from firefighting.

A TYPICAL DAY

No two days are the same for firefighters. Firefighters do not even work regular hours. Some work 48-hour shifts at a time and each shift brings new challenges. This is what one 24-hour shift might be like, if there were no emergency calls.

A FIREFIGHTER'S DAY

- **8 a.m.** Firefighters line up for **roll call** and to get their schedule for the day, which will include the duties and training they will have between calls.
- **8:15 a.m.** The first job is checking, repairing, and cleaning all the equipment.
- **9:30 a.m.** Firefighters live in the fire station for long stretches of time, so in the mornings they clean their living quarters, too.
- **10 a.m.** Work out! Firefighters must be fit and strong so they try to spend time in the gym every day.
- **11 a.m.** Before lunch, firefighters do jobs like collecting food and other supplies.
- **1 p.m.** After lunch, firefighters take part in activities that include training, **fire-safety inspections**, public education sessions, and station tours.
- **6 p.m.** After dinner and until bedtime, many of the firefighters on duty complete reports on fire or emergency **incidents**, work on special projects, or study for tests.

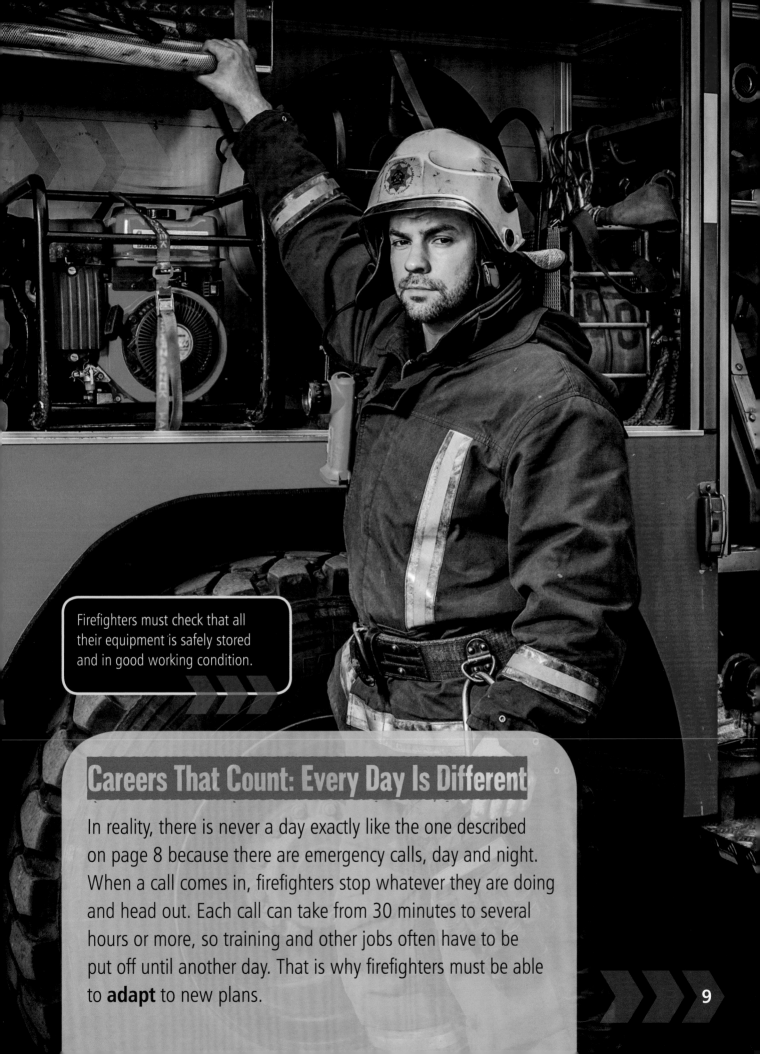

Firefighters must check that all their equipment is safely stored and in good working condition.

Careers That Count: Every Day Is Different

In reality, there is never a day exactly like the one described on page 8 because there are emergency calls, day and night. When a call comes in, firefighters stop whatever they are doing and head out. Each call can take from 30 minutes to several hours or more, so training and other jobs often have to be put off until another day. That is why firefighters must be able to **adapt** to new plans.

EQUIPMENT

The one job that must be done every day without fail, no matter how many calls there are, is checking the equipment. Firefighting equipment must be working properly at all times. How well it works could be the difference between life and death.

Fire engines are large trucks that can carry firefighting crews, equipment, and water to the scene of an emergency. Crews ride in the cab at the front and tools are kept in lockers on the sides. On the back is a turntable ladder that can turn in all directions. It also has sections that can extend to reach tall buildings.

Firefighters rely on equipment like these long ladders to get the job done and to keep safe.

WHAT MAKES A GREAT FIREFIGHTER?

Firefighters work with a lot of technology, including **thermal imagers**, **satellite** maps, computers, and other digital equipment. The equipment helps firefighters predict wind directions and access information needed to **monitor** and fight fires. Do you think understanding how the equipment works is as important as being fit enough to fight fires?

helmet

mask

flashlight

protective suit

thermal imaging camera

ax

Among the axes, hoses, **fire extinguishers**, and other equipment on board a fire engine, firefighters also have **oxygen** tanks and thermal imagers, or thermal imaging cameras. Burning buildings are filled with smoke and poisonous gases that make it hard to see and can choke people. Firefighters wear masks to protect their faces. They also carry a tank of clean air that they breathe in through a tube fitted to the mask. Firefighters use thermal imaging cameras to see through smoke and darkness so they can search for victims trapped in fires.

ALL SYSTEMS GO!

When an emergency happens, an alarm sounds in the fire station and the details and location of the incident flash onto a computer screen. Then it is all systems go for the firefighters!

Firefighters change into uniform within seconds. Uniforms are stored hanging up so firefighters can put them on quickly. The uniform is vital for safety. It has:

- Fasteners made of Velcro, which are easy to close.

- A tough, plastic helmet to protect the head.

- A thick waterproof and fireproof jacket covered in **reflective** strips.

- Thick waterproof and fireproof boots with steel toes to protect feet from falling **debris**. The boots also have solid soles in case firefighters step on something sharp.

In the fire engine, a map flashes up on a screen for the driver to follow. Another crew member stays on the radio for updates from the station. The fire engine moves quickly, so its noisy siren warns other drivers to get out of the way. As the fire engine speeds through the streets, the firefighters prepare themselves for what they might find at the scene.

Firefighters race to their engines and speed through the streets to get to the scene of a fire quickly.

Careers That Count: Knowing the Local Area

Firefighters have to take time to get to know local streets and buildings around their fire station so that they can respond to emergency calls **efficiently**.

FIGHTING FIRES

Every fire is unique and firefighters have to fight different fires in different ways. However, one rule remains the same whatever the fire. Firefighters must deprive the fire of one of the three things it needs: **fuel**, oxygen, or heat.

Firefighters use hoses from a water tank or from a street **hydrant** to spray cold water onto the fire. Hoses have pumps that can spray water 300 feet (91 m) away, or more. It can take several firefighters to hold a hose because it sprays water forcefully. Firefighters remove fuel, the wood, and other **flammable** materials in a building by spraying foam or powder to stop oxygen spreading. They also use axes to remove walls and roofs. Firefighters may stand on a platform at the top of the ladder to spray roofs or to reach people trapped in tall buildings.

firefighters holding a hose

WHAT MAKES A GREAT FIREFIGHTER?

Firefighters need to be practical and they also need to be able to understand how fires work. They study the science of fires to understand them better. How do you think this knowledge might help them better respond to fires?

Careers That Count: Firefighting Roles

At the scene of a fire, firefighters work under a commanding officer and have specific jobs to do. Hose operators connect the hoses to fire hydrants and aim the water toward the fire. The pump operators control the water flow. Other firefighters guide the extended ladders or enter burning buildings to rescue victims.

Firefighters work in teams. The firefighter at the top of a ladder relies on one in the fire engine to control where the ladder goes.

CRASH RESCUE

Fighting fires is only about 20 percent of what a firefighter does. Firefighters also answer requests to attend other emergencies, like traffic accidents. Firefighters go to traffic accidents because there are often fires at the scene or injured people trapped in vehicles.

As soon as firefighters arrive at a crash site, they check for safety. They first make sure that vehicles are not leaking dangerous fluids or are on fire. Then they put up warnings to keep other drivers clear of the area. To rescue someone trapped in a vehicle as quickly as possible, they explain to the victim what is happening and use a **tarp** to protect him or her from debris. The firefighters may use a wide variety of hand tools and mechanical equipment, like **hydraulic spreaders** and cutters, special saws, winches, and rams, to safely break open a vehicle.

firefighter's ax

Careers That Count: Fit to Fight Fires

Firefighters often have to move heavy objects, operate heavy equipment, and carry victims from damaged vehicles or burning buildings while wearing heavy safety gear. Being in top physical shape is absolutely essential for those following a career in firefighting.

WHAT MAKES A GREAT FIREFIGHTER?

Sometimes firefighters are the first at an emergency scene, like a car accident in which there are **multiple fatalities**. Facing situations like these can be emotionally challenging. How do you think firefighters prepare themselves to cope with some of the distressing duties they are asked to perform?

Firefighters use powerful tools like these to cut through metal and release victims trapped in cars and other vehicles.

FOREST FIREFIGHTERS

Forest fires and other wildfires are very dangerous. Winds can make a fire spread quickly and change direction without warning. Forest fires can also go on for days or weeks, so firefighters may work without time off for long periods. Being a forest firefighter is tough and challenging, and it can sometimes be a frightening job.

Helicopters are used to deliver firefighters and their equipment to forest fires and to drop water over areas of fire.

WHAT MAKES A GREAT FIREFIGHTER?

Firefighters use a variety of tools, both hand tools and power tools. It is important to be able to understand how these work and how to use them. How do you think these tools could help firefighters deal with emergency situations, like car accidents or burning buildings?

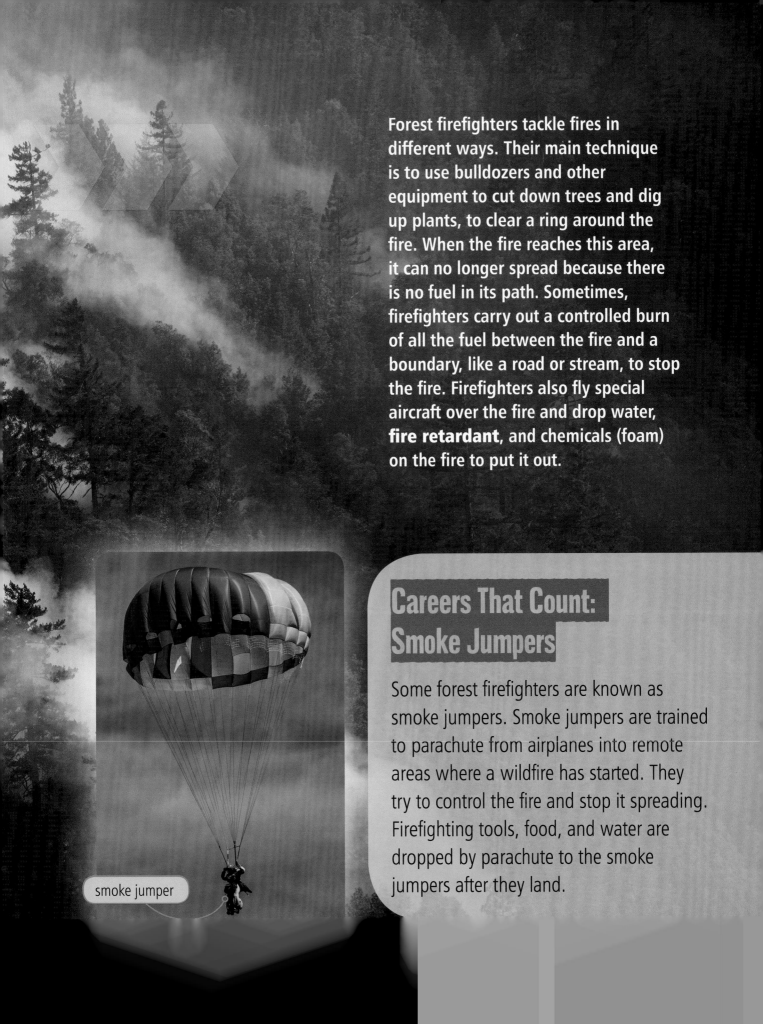

Forest firefighters tackle fires in different ways. Their main technique is to use bulldozers and other equipment to cut down trees and dig up plants, to clear a ring around the fire. When the fire reaches this area, it can no longer spread because there is no fuel in its path. Sometimes, firefighters carry out a controlled burn of all the fuel between the fire and a boundary, like a road or stream, to stop the fire. Firefighters also fly special aircraft over the fire and drop water, **fire retardant**, and chemicals (foam) on the fire to put it out.

smoke jumper

Careers That Count: Smoke Jumpers

Some forest firefighters are known as smoke jumpers. Smoke jumpers are trained to parachute from airplanes into remote areas where a wildfire has started. They try to control the fire and stop it spreading. Firefighting tools, food, and water are dropped by parachute to the smoke jumpers after they land.

DISASTER!

Firefighters are also called to help after bomb incidents, hurricanes, floods, or other disasters. These calls are especially challenging as firefighters often have to think of new ways to tackle such emergencies.

Hazmat suits cover a firefighter's whole body to protect him or her from hazardous materials.

Careers That Count: Controlling Danger

Some firefighters work in **hazardous materials units.** They are specially trained to control and clean up dangerous materials at oil spills and chemical accidents. By doing so, they protect citizens from exposure to hazardous substances. They wear special **hazmat suits** and use equipment to identify different dangerous substances.

In a disaster situation, there may be injured people trapped in burning houses, collapsed roads and buildings, and hazardous waters. Cables and pipes may be damaged, leaving the area without power and with the danger of more explosions or shocks. Firefighters work as part of a **task force**, alongside other rescue services and engineers, medics, and other specialists. They put out fires, rescue people, move large debris to make way for rescues, and inspect sites for dangers like gas leaks. They also help clean up and check sites after dealing with the incident.

WHAT MAKES A GREAT FIREFIGHTER?

At the scene of a disaster, a lot can be happening at once. Firefighters need to cooperate and get along with a wide range of people in their crews and other emergency services. Their lives and the lives of other people depend on it. What other qualities do you think firefighters need to be good team players?

Firefighters help people in different kinds of emergencies, including earthquakes and hurricanes.

MEDICAL AID

As part of helping to protect people and places, firefighters may also have the responsibility of providing emergency medical care at the site of an incident. They are often first to arrive at a scene, and knowing how to treat injured victims immediately saves countless lives.

A large number of a fire department's emergency responses are calls for medical aid, for things like accidents at home and work or injuries resulting from car crashes. Firefighters are trained to give first aid, such as bandaging wounds. They also treat patients for things that are life-threatening. For example, they will give **CPR** to someone who is not breathing properly or is suffering a heart attack.

Careers That Count: Qualified to Save Lives

Almost all fire departments require firefighters to be **certified** as **emergency medical technicians (EMTs)**. Some require firefighters to be certified as **paramedics**. Paramedics receive more advanced training and can perform some procedures and give some medications that EMTs cannot.

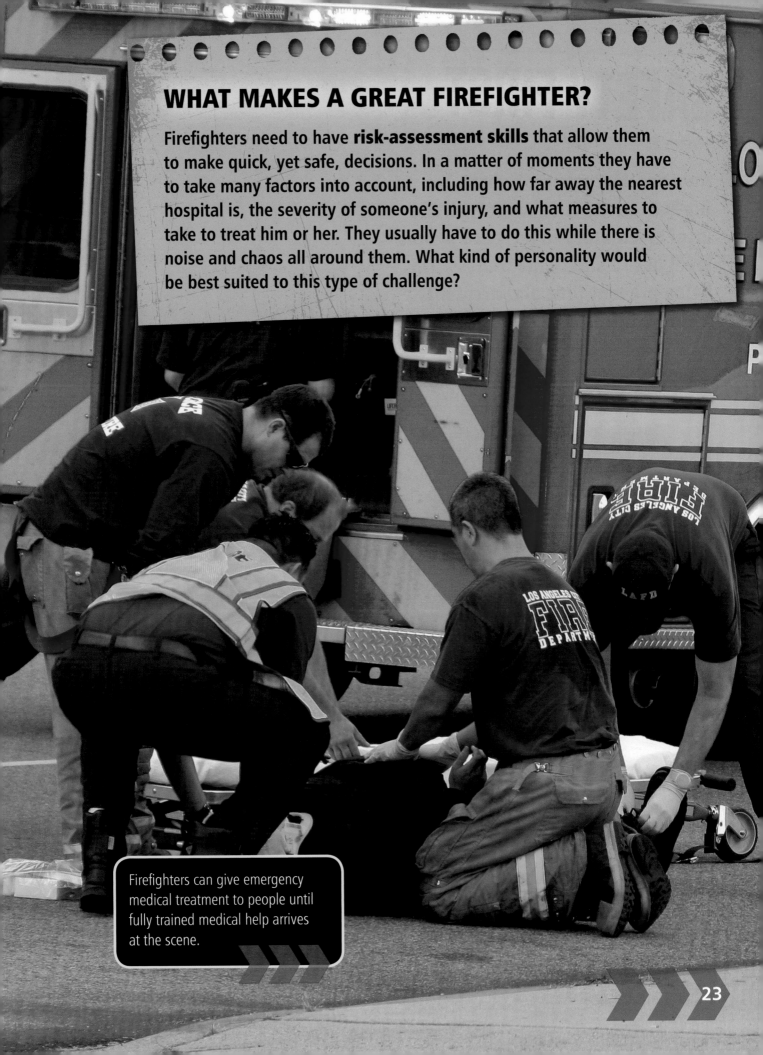

WHAT MAKES A GREAT FIREFIGHTER?

Firefighters need to have **risk-assessment skills** that allow them to make quick, yet safe, decisions. In a matter of moments they have to take many factors into account, including how far away the nearest hospital is, the severity of someone's injury, and what measures to take to treat him or her. They usually have to do this while there is noise and chaos all around them. What kind of personality would be best suited to this type of challenge?

Firefighters can give emergency medical treatment to people until fully trained medical help arrives at the scene.

SAFETY FIRST

Another important job that firefighters do is to work with the local community to increase people's level of fire-safety awareness. This helps prevent fires and accidents from occurring in the first place.

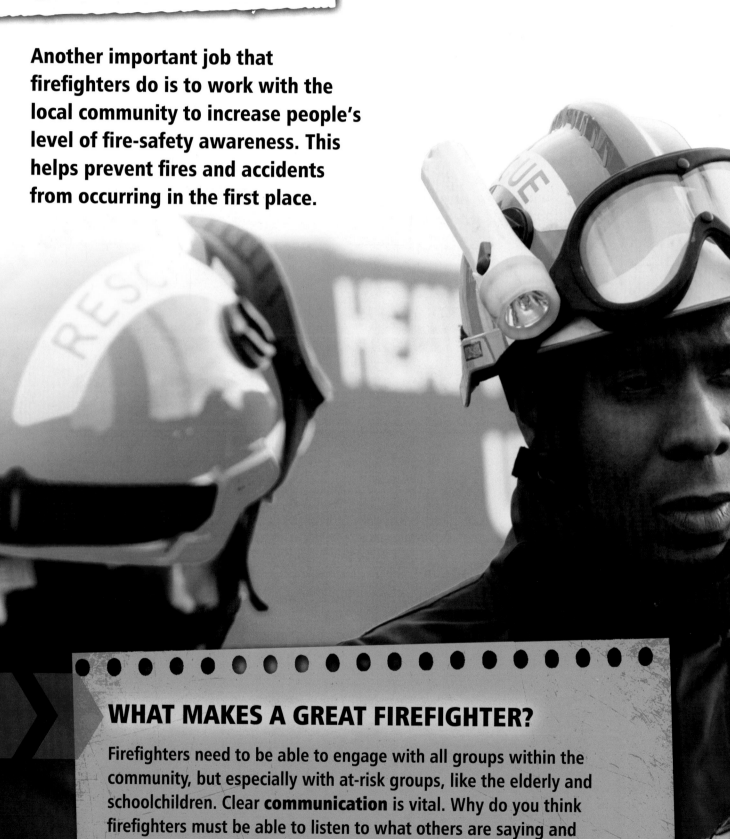

WHAT MAKES A GREAT FIREFIGHTER?

Firefighters need to be able to engage with all groups within the community, but especially with at-risk groups, like the elderly and schoolchildren. Clear **communication** is vital. Why do you think firefighters must be able to listen to what others are saying and explain information clearly?

Firefighters educate the public in different ways. They visit schools and community centers to give talks and presentations about what to do if there is a fire. They explain how people should get out of a burning building, stay out, and call the emergency number. They talk to people about safety at home and the importance of smoke alarms. Firefighters talk about fire safety and enforce fire-safety standards in public and business places. For example, they advise people about alarms and sprinkler systems and check that safety features, like fire escapes, work well.

Careers That Count: Investigating Fires

Some firefighters become fire investigators. They find where the fire started and they look for evidence if **arson** is suspected. They figure out how a fire began and they may have to testify in court if, for example, a fire happened because a company did not follow fire-safety rules.

Part of a firefighter's job is helping to make communities more aware of fire safety issues.

RISKS AND REWARDS

Firefighting is a tough business. In fact, it is one of the most challenging and dangerous of careers. So, why do firefighters do it?

Firefighters are constantly rushing into unknown situations in which they might be injured or killed. They often face dangers that include collapsing floors and walls, traffic accidents, and exposure to smoke and flames. However, firefighters are highly trained and they work with excellent safety equipment, which lessens the risks of the job. Firefighters are confident in their training and want to do what they can to help. Their reward is the feeling of satisfaction and accomplishment that comes from saving someone's life or property.

Careers That Count: Always Learning

Firefighters never stop learning and training. Attending lectures, doing practice drills, and following other training courses are an important part of the job. Training takes place throughout a firefighter's career. Firefighters need to master many skills and need to keep updating and adding to them.

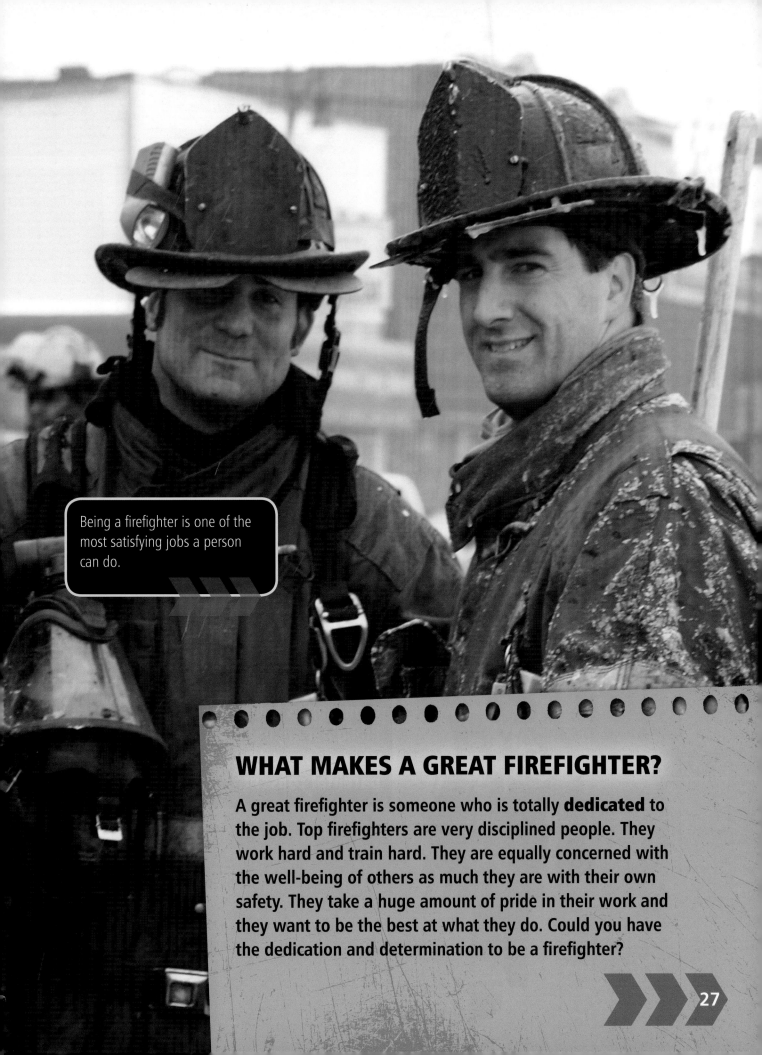

Being a firefighter is one of the most satisfying jobs a person can do.

WHAT MAKES A GREAT FIREFIGHTER?

A great firefighter is someone who is totally **dedicated** to the job. Top firefighters are very disciplined people. They work hard and train hard. They are equally concerned with the well-being of others as much they are with their own safety. They take a huge amount of pride in their work and they want to be the best at what they do. Could you have the dedication and determination to be a firefighter?

COULD YOU HAVE A CAREER THAT COUNTS?

Do you want to become a firefighter? Following these steps will help you reach your goal.

Subjects to study at school: You do not need to study particular subjects, but math, science, engineering, and technology will be useful. Take opportunities to practice teamwork while at school, and to mix and deal with people from a wide range of backgrounds.

Work experience: Become a volunteer firefighter. Many communities have a volunteer firefighter organization you can join at 16, with **parental consent**.

Exams to pass: You need to have a high school diploma or a GED to apply to be a firefighter.

College: You do not have to get a college degree because firefighters mainly train on the job, but some colleges offer a fire service pre-recruitment course. A degree in fire science or fire technology or even math, chemistry, biology, communication skills, or computer literacy can improve your chances of employment.

Life experience: Get fit and stay fit. Firefighters have to be physically fit and have to pass a medical examination before they will be accepted. They must pass their driver's license test, too.

Improve your résumé: Volunteer in your community. Do not volunteer just to increase your chances of getting a job, but because you have a real interest in caring for your fellow citizens. You do not have to do something fire-related, just show that you want to care for people in your community.

Getting the job: Applicants are expected to pass written, physical, and medical examinations prior to being considered for a job. Once you have been hired, you will also do physical training exercises and get medical training, for example, the EMT certificate.

GLOSSARY

adapt To change in order to cope with a new situation.

ambitions Hopes and goals.

arson The criminal act of deliberately setting fire to property.

career adviser A person trained to help people find out which career is best for them.

certified Recognized as being fully qualified to do something.

characteristics Features or qualities belonging to a particular person or thing.

communication The giving and receiving of information.

CPR An acronym for cardiopulmonary resuscitation. CPR is a first aid technique that can be used if someone is not breathing properly or if his or her heart has stopped.

criminal record A record of the crimes a person has committed.

debris The bits and pieces scattered at the scene of an accident or other incident.

dedicated Devoted and completely committed to something.

efficiently Well and quickly.

emergency medical technicians (EMTs) Health care providers of emergency medical services.

excluded Not allowed to take part.

fire extinguishers Portable devices that discharge a jet of water, foam, gas, or other material to extinguish a fire.

fire retardant A substance that makes fuels less likely to catch fire or slows down how quickly they catch fire.

fire-safety inspections Checks carried out to be sure an area is not at risk of fire.

flammable Easily set on fire.

fuel A substance that creates heat when it is burned.

hazardous materials units Teams that are trained to deal with dangerous substances.

hazmat suits Rubber and plastic coverings that protect people from harmful chemicals and other hazardous substances.

hydrant A water pipe, usually in a street, with a nozzle to which a fire hose can be attached.

hydraulic spreaders Tools used by emergency rescue workers to break open vehicles or other spaces where people are trapped.

incidents Accidents or dangerous events.

medical record A record of all the health care a person has received.

monitor To check and watch something closely.

multiple fatalities Many deaths.

oxygen A gas found in the air.

paramedics People who have medical training to deal with injured people at accident sites.

parental consent Given approval by your parents to do something.

reflective A surface that light or heat bounces off.

rigorous Extremely thorough.

risk-assessment skills Skills that enable people to decide how dangerous a situation is.

roll call The process of calling out a list of names to establish who is present.

satellite A machine that is in orbit around the Earth. It collects, receives, and passes on information.

tarp A plastic covering.

task force A group given a specific task, or job, to do.

thermal imagers Devices that help people see in the dark.

FURTHER READING

Goldish, Meish. *Hotshots* (Fire Fight! The Bravest). New York, NY: Bearport Publishing, 2014.

Riddle, John. *Firefighter* (Careers With Character). Broomall, PA: Mason Crest, 2014.

Rogers, Brian. *Career As A Firefighter: What They Do, How to Become One, and What the Future Holds!* CreateSpace Independent Publishing Platform, 2013.

Royston, Angela. *Diary of a Firefighter.* North Mankato, MN: Capstone Publishing, 2013.

WEBSITES

Due to the changing nature of Internet links, PowerKids Press has developed an online list of websites related to the subject of this book. This site is updated regularly. Please use this link to access the list: **www.powerkidslinks.com/ctc/fire**

INDEX